Aleksander Wat

MEDITERRANEAN POEMS

Edited & translated by

Czeslaw Milosz

Ardis / Ann Arbor

Copyright © 1977 by Ardis

*Ardis World Poets in Translation Series,
No. 1*

ISBN 0-88233-205-8

CONTENTS

Foreword

My late friend Aleksander Wat had a picturesque life but he should not be envied by people less exposed to pranks of History. Born in 1900 in Warsaw, he belonged to a Polish intelligentsia family of Jewish origin. Among his ancestors he counted Rashi of Troyes, an eleventh century commentator on the Sacred Books; Isaac Luria, the great cabalist of the sixteenth century; and a great rabbi of Kutno, Gaon, whose tomb was believed to have miraculous powers. Wat's father studied the Kabbalah but also Plotinus and Kierkegaard, without trying, however, to influence his children who grew up as atheists and socialists. In his childhood Wat was strongly marked by the peasant piety of his family's Roman Catholic servant, nurse and friend, Anna Mikulak—and by innumerable books in his father's library. No wonder that as a young man he entered the University of Warsaw to study philosophy. Yet instead of becoming a philosopher he became a poet, a co-founder, in 1919, of the Polish futurist (in fact, rather dadaist) movement.

Soon he abandoned poetry for prose and in 1927 he published his collection of fantastic tales, *Lucifer Unemployed;* their topsy-turvy logic did not announce the political choice he was to make. But Wat, like many of his contemporaries, gradually turned into an admirer of the Russian Revolution and used to act as a host to Soviet writers visiting Warsaw in the twenties. He was a personal friend of Vladimir Mayakovsky who notes in his diaries: "Wat is a born futurist." The Polish Communist Party at that time had no legal existence but managed to publish some periodicals. Without being a Party member, Wat, a zealous Leftist, exhibited rare energy as the editor in chief of the most important Polish Communist magazine before World War II, "The Literary Monthly" ("Miesiecznik Literacki") which appeared from 1929 to 1932 (when it was closed down by the Polish authorities). A few months in prison followed, remembered by Wat as rather idyllic in comparison with his later prison experiences.

The thirties in Poland was a sad period full of dark forebodings and sterile for Wat as a creative writer. In 1939, fleeing the advancing German army, Wat found himself in the Eastern part of Poland, soon incorporated into the Soviet Union, and settled in the city of Lwow. Arrested in the beginning of 1940, he started his Odyssey through numerous prisons: Lwow, Kiev, Moscow (Lubianka), Saratov. The accusations ranged from Trotskyism and Zionism to being an agent of the Vatican. The people of all possible nationalities, creeds and backgrounds that he met during his prison years made for his true, as he used to say later, education. Released as a result of amnesty for the Poles (after Hitler's attack on Russia), he went to Alma-Ata in Kazakhstan where, as he had no permit to live in that city, he was kept clandestinely for a while in a hotel room by the famous Soviet literary scholar Victor Shklovsky whom he had befriended earlier. Several writers and film directors (Zoshchenko, Paustovsky, Eisenstein and others) evacuated from Moscow lived in Alma-Ata at that time (1942) and Wat frequented their private gatherings. His decision not to go to the side of the Union of Patriots (the nucleus of the future Polish Communist Goverment, then being organized in the Soviet Union) resulted in his banishment to Ili, a settlement in the Asian desert. His refusal to acquire Soviet citizenship brought about renewed imprisonment. He succeeded in returning to Poland in 1946 and began publishing his essays and poetry. Persecuted during the Stalinist years (1949-1956), however, he suffered a stroke and never completely recovered. His revival as a poet verges on the miraculous and he gave the full measure of his talent only in the last decade of his life, 1957-1967, when his illness grew worse each year. After 1956 he was extolled, awarded a literary prize and acclaimed by the young generation. He could now travel abroad and lived mostly in the south of France or in Italy, both because of the state of his health and his appraisal of the situation in Poland. He died in Paris in 1967.

His poetic work and his stories are not the only components of his *oeuvre*. For years he dreamed of writing a huge book-memoir, a sort of *summa* of his political and philosophical observations, his remembrance of things past. This proved to be impossible as his illness would leave him too few respites. But the book, though only the first volume has been published so far, exists, in the form of my interviews with him registered on tape during his prolonged stay in Berkeley in 1964-65 and during my stay in Paris.

Whether he was a "born futurist" or not, Wat is primarily a poet and what he wrote in the last period of his life secures a place for him in world literature as well as in the literature of his native country. His is a poetry of experience, of bitter wisdom, of great suffering in the most literal, physical sense. As such it will probably remain a permanent document of our century. The translations presented here are due to a large extent to the initiative and the cooperation of my students at the University of California in Berkeley. They liked Wat's kind of serious buffoonery: his very style, they used to say, makes us feel the whole weight of reality.

Czeslaw Milosz

MEDITERRANEAN POEMS

I

BEFORE BREUGEL THE ELDER

Work is a blessing.
I tell you that, I—professional sluggard!
Who slobbered in so many prisons! Fourteen!
And in so many hospitals! Ten! And innumerable inns!
Work is a blessing.
How else could we deal with the lava of fratricidal love
                                        towards fellow men?
With those storms of extermination of all by all?
With brutality, bottomless and measureless?
With the black and white era which does not want to end
endlessly repeating itself da capo like a record
forgotten on a turntable
spinning by itself?
Or perhaps someone invisible watches over the phonograph? Horror!
How, if not for work, could we live in the paradise of
                                        social hygienists
who never soak their hands in blood without aseptic gloves?
Horror!
How else could we cope with death?
That Siamese sister of life
who grows together with it—in us, and is extinguished with it
and surely for that reason is ineffective.
And so we have to live without end,
without end. Horror!
How, if not for work, could we cope with ineffective death
(Do not scoff!)
which is like a sea,
where everyone is an Icarus, one of nearly three billion,
and, besides, so much happens all around us
and everything is equally unimportant, precisely, unimportant
although so difficult, so inhumanly difficult, so painful!
How then could we cope with all that?

Work is our rescue.
I tell you that—I, Breughel, the Elder (and I, for one,
your modest servant, Wat, Aleksander)-work is our rescue.

Saint—Mandé, July 1956

TO BE A MOUSE

To be a mouse. Preferably a field mouse. Or a garden mouse—
but not the kind that live in houses.
Man exhales an abominable smell!
We all know it—birds, crabs, rats.
He provokes disgust and fear.
    Trembling.

To feed on wisteria flowers, on the bark of palm trees,
to dig up roots in cold, humid soil
and to dance after a fresh night. To look at the full moon,
to reflect in one's eyes the sleek light of lunar
    Agony.

To burrow in a mouse hole for the time when wicked Boreas
will search for me with his cold, bony fingers
in order to squeeze my little heart under the
                    blade of his claw,
a cowardly mouse heart—
    A palpitating crystal.

Menton—Garavan, April 1956

FROM PERSIAN PARABLES

By a great, swift water
on a stony bank
a human skull was lying
and shouting: Allah la ilah.

And in that cry such horror
and such supplication
so great was its despair
that I asked the helmsman:

For what can it still cry out? Of what is it still afraid?
What divine judgment could strike it yet again?

Suddenly there came a wave
took hold of the skull
and tossing it about
smashed it against the bank.

Nothing is ultimate
—the helmsman's voice was hollow—
and there is no bottom to evil.

A FLAMINGO'S DREAM

Water water water. And nothing but water.
If only one inch of land! An inch of no—matter—what land!
To set one foot on! If only!

We begged the gods for that! All of them!
Water gods, land gods, southern gods, northern gods,
For an inch, a strip, a scrap of any kind of land!
No more than just enough to support the claw of one foot!
And nothing. Only water. Nothing except water.
Water water water.
If only a speck of land!
There is no salvation.

IMAGERIE D'EPINAL

On the death of Reik, Slansky and thousands of others.

The executioner yawned. From his axe the blood was still dripping.
"Don't cry, here's a lollipop, don't, my child."

He took her in his arms. Carressed her. And she
                                        looked at the head.
At the sightless eyes. At the dumb lips.

It was the head of her father. Later on, embalmed,
washed, it was put on a pole and nicely painted.

With that pole she marched in a parade on a sunny, populous road,
under her school placard:
                "Happiness for all—death to enemies..."

1949

X was asked
     if he believed in the objective existence of Parzota
—To believe in the objective existence of Parzota—
     (that) smacks of mysticism,
I am an old horse, you know, and a staunch
rationalist—
answered X.
The sequel was more interesting.

X persisted in his refusal to believe in the
                        objective existence of
   Parzota.
Who, the said Parzota, placed him in a dungeon,
                 put him to torture.
Yet everything would have been in perfect order
if not for one sad circumstance:
the stupid man of principle was so obstinate that
                 he died in the dungeon.
Poor Parzota! Condemned to eternal doubt.
Now he will never find out
if he existed objectively.

1953

A DAMNED MAN

First in my dream appeared a coffee mill.
Most ordinary. The oldfashioned kind. A coffee-brown color.
(As a child, I liked to slide open the lid, peek in and instantly
snap it shut. With fear and trembling! So that my
                              teeth chattered with terror.
It was as if I myself were being ground up in there! I always knew
I would come to a bad end!)
So first there was a coffee mill.
Or perhaps I only imagined it, because a moment later
                              a windmill stood there.
And that windmill stood on the sea, on the sea,
                    on the horizon's line, in its very center.
Its four wings turned creaking and cracking. They
                    were probably grinding somebody up
And at the tip of every one of them
an equilibrist in white
revolved to the melody of "The Merry Widow",
supported by his left hand resting on the wing he
                         floated, fiery, fluid, fleeting,
a silver flame fluttering his feet in the ether.
Then he waned. And so one after the other. It would have
                    been dark if not for a burning moon.
Oh, where did they come from? Equestriennes?! My
                         marvellous equestriennes!
Lightly on heavy but swift percherons
they gallop one after another and I see crowds, crowds of them—
some in ruffles of tulle, others naked, stark naked
                         in black silk stockings,
still others in beads—golden, turquoise, black and iridescent,
and their thighs white like sugar! Like teeth! And
                    strong, o mighty God, how strong!
(As a young boy I dreamed: an equestrienne—only an equestrienne!
will saddle the great love in my life! Well, I've never met one.

11

And it's probably better that way, for what a couple we would
                                have made: an equestrienne
and a bookkeeper in a nationalized funeral parlor.)
Well, nothing lasts forever. Since a moment later
instead of the equestriennes, Sabines were parading, armored
                                women, much more vulgar after all
(eleven years ago I fell in love with a certain Sabina,
a divorcee, alas without reciprocity).
Thus the Sabines
never carried away, but, let me concede, ravishing. Taking me where?
Where? How can I know where?
In any case—towards annihilation.

I woke up. I always knew I would come to a bad end.

AT THE EXHIBIT

Our world. So small
That one guitar
is enough
to populate it with sounds—
if played by Love.

Love is not seen
though it is present.

Beside the guitar a patera with apples
—a mark of royalty
known from the tarot;
the realization of evil-good;
the fruit of the Hesperides
but not made of gold,
on the contrary—of colors
from our world
which is so small
that one guitar is enough
etc.

All this is seen
except Love
which is not seen
though it is present
in a small exhibit
of a picture dealer
on Faubourg Saint-Honorè.

Paris, December 1955

If the word "exists" is to have any meaning
it should refer to something to which we can return.
Yet there is no return! Everything is once
and before it has begun to "exist", it has already ceased to "exist"
(Notice: "has begun" and "has ceased" are equally unfounded)
and the alternation "is" and "is not" is not a sequence of time,
it unfolds itself beyond time—insofar as "unfolds"
can be used here.
Therefore
let us turn again to essence. For with it we are more certain.
Since we create it ourselves. It is not dependent
either upon whether it "is" or whether it "is not".

How good it is to return to old rejected concepts!
(N.B. The meaning of that "let us return" is
                                    common. So, for example,
Odysseus returned to Penelope, to her who knew the secret:
that one must weave and unweave. And again weave and unweave.)

ARITHMETIC

When you are alone
don't think you are alone.
He (she) is always with you.

Anywhere you go
you are always followed.
The most faithful dog is not so faithful,
a shadow sometimes disappears,
he (she)—never.

That red-haired whore is leaning against the doorway of a hotel
and with her is—not her double—she, another she.
That old man sneaks in after her like a cat
and with him is his inseparable companion.

Those two on a bed in contortions.
These two sit at the foot and wait, sadly hanging their heads.

Paris, June 1956

IN A BAR, SOMEWHERE NEAR SÈVRES-BABYLONE

(From Parisian kitsch)

At the counter a slut was sitting. She kept her eyes fixed
on a glass from which she drew, with a straw, a ruby liquor.
Not very young, but not old. Sturdy. Brutal features,
yet character dressed them in dignity, even nobility.
It was still winter. The morning was marvelous, sunny.
Paris disentangled itself from iridescent aquamarine mist.
In the window a little church across the square. Where bells
happened to be chiming.
I do not know for what reason.

The woman raised her eyelids. Like a ballet-dancer
who lifts herself on tiptoes. But her dun-yellow pupils
were petrified. And yet they concealed inside
a flicker or perhaps a light—
a light imprisoned in amber.
This made her resemble a Cumaean Sybilla
seated on a stool at a counter, her legs spread apart.

She swept the room with a casually professional look,
sized up two old men bent over their dominoes
and hesitated suddenly when meeting my eyes—
uncertain whether I would be a timid aspirant
to her breasts, hard and robust, to her legs, chopped in stone,
in black open-work, fin-de-siècle, stockings.
(Where did she find them in our era of nylon,
she, a model of Toulouse-Lautrec's,
a Babylonian whore?)

But soon recognized her mistake, slowly retracted her eyes,
covered them with thick eyelids as with a lampshade of tin.
And again fixed her pupils on the very tall glass
from which she drew with a straw blood-ruby liquor.

16

The bells of the little church chimed more and more insistently,
in a mirror my face looked at me, here some-what alien, not-mine.

From the street through the half-open door two big cats walked in,
step by step following each other, stalking cautiously, slowly —
both fat and dirty-gray. Swinging their tails in rhythm
as soldiers in a parade swing their arms, unaware of onlookers.
They came up to the woman, rubbed against her legs,
then lazily lay down on both sides of the tabouret —
you would say: two sphynxes drowsing on guard at a sullen tomb.

Severe tension departed from her indurate face.
To relax.
That was, for a while, happiness.

A TURTLE FROM OXFORD

To K. Jelenski

And when the queen of Sheba heard of
the fame of Solomon concerning the name
of the Lord, she came to prove him with
hard questions.
I Kings, 10.

On the eastern sidewalk of Magdalen College a small
turle reflected a long time before he answered
my question, he moved his jaws like a meccano: "That
even I cannot remember: I am hardly
two hundred and ninety-three. But in our family
a record has been preserved how our ancestor, of blessed memory,
assisted at the loves of the queen of Sheba with
                                        your great-grandfather.
As to the riddles she presumably asked him to solve, our tradition
is silent. What is known: it occurred in a wine-colored chamber
where, instead of lamps, gold was shining, from Tyre, no doubt.
My ancestor, was not a learned turtle, a respectable one,
for certain..."

With short steps we shuffled after him, I, my beautiful
wife and Adriana, our charming guide.
We listened to the turtle solemnly. When he lost his breath
my wife with a kind stroke of her finger
animated his little snout. After all, that's why I wander!
In strange lands! In my old age!
I write, that is to say, my autobiography and gather data
for the geneology of our ancient stock. An English duke
brought the turtle to my attention, in a waterfront dive in Naples
in return for a bowl of spaghetti and a glass
of wine ("My great-great-grandfather, an admiral,
took that turtle to Oxford all the way from Abyssinia").
Thus all three of us listened to the turtle with the solemnity due

to a dignified university person. This time
the pause was irritatingly long when all of a sudden,
from behind an island, young laughter was heard
and a boat passed, carrying a couple away.
Neither of them graceful. But my wife was delighted
to hear laughter of lovers. There is no need to add
that tiptoeing after the turtle and straining to hear
what he might deign to tell us, we were bent so low
that one may say we were on all fours.
Were they laughing at this? At their love?
At love in general? It does not matter.

                         "So, hardly had
he turned over on his back when he asked: 'And *now*
tell me, baby, what do they think of me in your country?'
The queen, still in rapture: 'That you love wisdom,'
she faltered, 'and women.' 'Wisdom?' he replied, 'I don't deny.
But women? Hardly. I love femininity.' "

Again there was a pause. This time not laughter but crying
and that of an infant, indeed, more bizarre here
than for instance a drunkard's railing in a cathedral.

                        "And he was right"
the turtle added at last. "He was wrong!" exclaimed
charming Adriana, blushing all over. She never interrupted
her elders, since she was a true young lady. "He was right,"
the turtle repeated, as though he had not heard. "A great lord
should love only universals: grassiness but not grass,
not humans but humanity, and arsiness but not..."

                        Whether he finished or not
I don't know, for Adriana again interjected, it is true, somewhat
abashed: "He who never loved someone, knows no love
at all." The turtle fell silent, for good; now he had taken
offense: nobody here had dared to contradict him.
We had no flies or anything else to smooth over the incident.
But my wife, who has a way with animals

and children, gently massaged his jowls.
So he spoke again, this time even garrulous:

"When King Solomon rolled off the queen for the third time,
he asked: 'Now, what counsel do your people ask for?
What do they want from me?' 'A toenail,' answered
the queen of Sheba, 'from the little toe of your foot.'
'I'll give it to them,' agreed the king and himself
handed her a pair of nail scissors. She pulled out a golden cup
artfully engraved by the hand of Hiram-Abi
which the king after their first intercourse had presented to her,
with a tight lid, upon it was carved the grim face of Ashtoreth.
A short cry, blood spurted into the cup, the lid slams...
What happened next, our ancestor did not relate.
Perhaps the whole thing so tired him, the strain upon his eyes,
upon his attention, that he suddenly fell asleep.
He was not learned. Who, after all, in those times,
was learned?"

                              "But what happened to the cup?
The cup?" I asked hollowly. For just then
a thought disturbed me, that perhaps
if I drink the blood of my ancestor
youth, eternal, wisdom, forever, will be restored to me!

                       "Oh yes," the turtle replied impassively,
"we know. The ship carrying the queen back, sank. Thirteen
Centuries later Senegalese sailors extracted the cup
from the belly of a whale, on the Indian ocean. "Undamaged?"
"Undamaged." Again a pause. "From Abyssinia, an Italian airman
Stole it together with the treasure of the King of Kings
not long ago...His plane fell into Etna."
"Into Etna!" I cried in falsetto, I straightened up
as well as I could and I raised my arms into the air,
frightening by this motion two male cardinals
that were fighting a knightly battle
on the grass, plucking at each other's beautiful scarlet crests.

20

"And yet Etna threw back the cup,"
unexpectedly screeched the turtle. "Like a
                              sandal?" "Of Empedocles,"
he asserted with a vivid satisfaction. Again silence. The crying
of the infant had long subsided. And the laugh of the lovers.
And the hissing of the birds. I could not stand this pause.
"Where is the blood of my ancestor?" I shouted, full of hope.

                              "Blood, blood, blood,"
he grated angrily. Adriana got up: "I wanted, master,
to sit at your feet and imbibe the words of wisdom from your
lips. And now..." she sobbed, poor, dear Adriana. "Blood,
of blood, with blood," repeated the turtle, obviously unable to stop.
"You gulped the blood of my cousins, is not that enough? Seizing
them in whole fistfuls in the bulrushes by the river Ili, crushing and
smashing them with a rolling pin, on the rough table in the kitchen
of the Prokombinat where you helped the dirty woman cook to
steal food. The blood of my brothers splashed into your eyes,
bespattered your face, your rags, you waded in their blood, still you
had not enough. You have never had enough. Not
                              enough. Not enough. Not
enough..."

I was afraid that he would have a stroke, he was choking.
Ashamed, we fled across the lawns and for a long time
the gargoyles of Magdalen pursued us with their howling laughter.

Oxford, July 1962

21

JAPANESE ARCHERY

1.
The hand tells the bowstring:
   Obey me.

The bowstring answers the hand:
   Draw Valiantly

The bowstring tells the arrow:
   O arrow, fly.

The arrow answers the bowstring:
   Speed my flight.

The arrow tells the target:
   Be my light.

The target answers the arrow:
   Love me.

2.
The target tells arrow, bowstring, hand and eye:
   Ta twam asi.

Which means in a sacred tongue:
   I am Thou.

3.
(Footnote of a Christian:
   O Mother of God,

watch over the target, the bow, the arrow
   and the archer).

Translated by Richard Lourie

* * *

To Leopold Labedz

...frisst der Grimm seine Gestaltungen in sich hinein.
Hegel

What can I do if for you I am
lumen obscurum? Believe me, in myself
I contain my whole self as a bright point.
Even transparent. But
                     a misunderstanding,
semantic, today reigns over all and sundry.

Do not forget though, my Hippolyte:
we are both well-behaved boys
in straw hats and white blouses
with navy-blue trim, who early in the morning
went chasing butterflies. But who, at nightfall
run after zigzags of lightning,
panting, exhausted. In vain ...
                 For not even those zigzags
will tear through Chaos! Nothing will tear Chaos
apart. It tears itself apart. Eating into
itself, piece after   piece,   insa-
tiated.
      And there's nothing I can do about it,
dear friend.

Paris, July 1963

23

II.

SONGS OF A WANDERER

"Ich stech das Licht. Ich stech das Licht
Ich stech das Hertz das ich liebe"
Schönwerth. *Aus der Oberplatz:
Sitten und Sagen.*

I.

For whom is the garden fated?
Who is happy there?
Whose eyes will be my haven?
Someone steals toward me.
What falls in the abyss?
A scream resounds.
A hand gropes upward.
Give me your hand, my son.
Wife, look into my eyes.

II.

Disgusted by everything alive I withdrew into the stone world: here
I thought, liberated, I would observe from above, but
                              without pride, those things
entangled in chaos. With the eyes of a stone, myself
                    a stone among stones, and like them sensitive,
pulsating to the turning of the sun. Retreating into
                         the depth of myself-stone,
motionless, silent; growing cold; present through a waning
                              of presence—in the cold
attractions of the moon. Like sand diminishing in
                              an hour-glass, evenly,
Ceaselessly, uniformly, grain by grain. Thus I shall be submitted
only to the rhythms of day and night. But—
no dance in them, no whirling, no frenzy: only
                              monastic rule, and silence.

They do not become, they are. Nothing else. Nothing
else, I thought, loathing
all which becomes.
I, a stone among stones. O, never had I thought
of stone in the words of death. I had always felt in it
a heart, a pulsation
of its life, and not just in its internal structures, which amaze
onlookers, photographers, mineralogists.... Simply:
the heart of a stone: Simply:
the dreams of a stone. To be in the heart of a stone—
how much I desired this!
In the heart of a stone, without the flaw which
through our tainted veins
slushes deep into our hearts and grows, making them
totally putrid matter,
subjected to all decay.
The dreams of a stone! how I
wanted to see the dreams
of a stone, through its own stony eyes! Perhaps
a human child, an infant.
when it is no longer a palpitating sponge of flesh,
but not yet—a man,
perhaps, in his eye, he retains a dream of a stone, not even a dream—
a reflection, an echo of a dream, distant and fading away. O,
how I wanted to be in the thought of a stone, to be what
its thought thinks. Or—
cursed in the beginning, exiled from stone, how I wanted to touch
the thought of a stone, just as I touch rose petals,
careful not to let it feel
my coarse, bulbous fingers, the fingers of a usurper:
it might die of disgust.
The thought of a stone, the thought of a
rose, what if they were akin?
in its very short season, when it is still folded-up wisdom,
and yet open to love; Eros, agapè—as I call this
in the obscure speech
of men, in speech without eyes, no—with eyes

repeatedly gouged out;
in snail words sent in whispers toward our cannibal lips
by our brain, which is nourished with blood, subjected to
rottenness, decay, putridity,
contaminating everything in its grasp with putridity, decay.
What's erosion, I thought,
to a stone? What's the crumbling of its inner structures?
The heart of a stone
is not in structures, in time-space relations? it is generous,
rebuilding structures, while time, impotent, disintegrates
them. The heart of a stone
does not submit to annihilation, to the death of everything which becomes.
Armored,
it is a sovereign monad.
I didn't envy the stone the
riches of its inner world.
I did not look for a shell to hide in, to gorge my mollusk
senses on the food of colors.
What are riches to the stone? Yes, in riches we surpassed
stones during our million-years' existence on earth. But
what are riches to them?
In their inner world nothing but poverty—as we call it,
using the gouged-out eyes
of our poor speech. But everything there is meaningful and pure,
everything there is everything.
Only there. If God exists, he is there. At the heart of stones.
Also—in their dreams.
Even the tree, the most perfect
creation of the demiurge
just before he fell asleep, when he was dozing on the
same edge above which
nods the head of a schoolboy, tired from poring over
a book on the table,
on that edge from which something irresistibly pulls
us down, into the dark, down and into the dark
from where we rose and rise obstinately—even the tree, I repeat,

28

when, like a strong man, it wedges into the stone and splits it apart
with its savage, dirt-covered, worm-coated root; when it
                                                            pulls out of mother earth
and without shame brings to light her magic dreams:
                                                            leaves, birds, grains,
even the tree, always prepared for flights, vibration,
                                                            frenzy—even the tree—
I repeat, the most beautiful creation of the demiurge
                                                            while on the edge of sleep—
what can it do to the stone?
                                    Perhaps, in the instant of his vertigo,
the wildest creature, in whom was set the terrifying spark of genius,
so desiring to die out! so unhappy is it in that dwelling-place—
                                                            perhaps man in vertigo
has a flash of intuition, when he approaches stones with pain,
                                                yet without noise, without pride?
a sculptor whose chisel, already lifted, is held back
                                                by the voice of the stone:
stop, here is your threshold, one scratch more and you will
                                                be rejected inexorably,
without return.
                        So I thought about stone. And
                                                since I loved everything
that is not even the negation of stone—but worse: otherness, all,
that is subjected to flaws, transience, death and—
                                                worse: resurrection
from death; and since I was sensuous to the marrow of my marrow,
since I loved my senses, my skin, all skin, every skin even unto
fiery hatred—the heart of a stone was closed to me,
sealed fast.
                        But now is the time of old age. Aetas
                                    serenitatis. Thus, disgusted
with the world of the living, its beauty turned toward
                                                death, decaying, rising
from the dead as vermin, as acrid weeds, as manure
                                                for peasant hands, thus
I fled into the stone world, in order—a stone among

stones, done with pride,
although from above—to slowly close my eyes, not yet
stony but no longer human,
to your sufferings, to your tenderness, to your
labors and those agonies
of yours, to all that is subjected to incessant putrefaction,
that is our torture, our shame, our shameful pity,
our beauty like radiant eyes in the face of a
hydrocephalic hunchback.

III.

So now, having fled into the stone world, I was slowly fal-
ling asleep, a stone under
my head, feeling how the warmth of its heart penetrates my head,
and makes it similar, its twin; when on the
edge of sleep, from where,
heavy with darkness we lean into greater darkness—now,
when I dreamt there: I, too,
am a stone among stones, and, like them, I am exalted
yet without pride, inert
and yet tense with strength, in a tense fullness which hangs
in the clenched stone fist
of the moon over a sterile landscape—
I was awakened by the din of those
whom I survived.
Remember! Remember!

Not in a double row did they surround me;
not in the carriage
of a survivor must I pass them; no holiday dresses do they wear:
no wreaths on their heads. Naked, though tightly
swathed in the lava
of clay. Like that one in Pompeii, who just managed
to lower his brow
lifted in amazement and to fix his tired death-stare on the earth

which betrayed him.

Remember! Remember! —They shout: and
they want to be forgotten.
Remember!—They shout: and they want eternal oblivion. Our hell—
is in the memory of those who will survive us.

Driven out by the din and the sham
of those whom I survived, I walked down through
rubble. And having lost
everything I knew in that difficult descent, I am again that
which I had been.

IV.

It is not erosion which crumbles stone here.

But the jaws of an old woman, whom
I pass on the road. A patient old woman, her eyes like cinders
under a dark-brown straw hat. What can atrophied jaws
crumble? Blind, this I see, but with her gnarled hand and
her olive walking stick
she gropes for her son's return from work. All in
expectation. So dwarfed
you would swear: she comes from a workshop of olivewood
holy figures. And time
tarnished her with its patina. She stands thus, on the
domestic threshold, bent
in two. The cold Mother Earth.

It is not erosion which crumbles stone
here. For the rot
is in its nature. To rot, to scale off, to disintegrate: this
is posited in the law
of minerals. In the law of mollusks. In the law of man.

Obstinate olive trees
dug into the earth walls of these cliffs; and deep
below—a vast trough.
It still keeps at bay upsurged waves of mountains,
once aroused against it

31

by the Vengeful Hand, when they were liquid, fiery,
                                crested. And thus
they petrified, barely humped, all in the same
crouch: henchmen waiting for the Master's sign.
The Vengeful Hand set them here as an eternal threat
above the mole and the bush, above the fretful ant,
                            above the young human
species, which secretes the glue of labor...
                    True, no man in sight: yet,
smoke from the farms. Yet, hamlets. Yet, highways, roads,
                            paths, in an incomprehensible
tangle. And—farther on—streams snake, coil in silver,
                            and far, far away
the navigable sea, and from under its shiny skin,
                            in this hour of luminescence
the skeletons of sunken ships project their afterglow. O yes,
water, also water, even water, so immaculate—
                            is contaminated, condemned;
for myriads of ages plasma crawls out of its floods,
                            in a relentless flow,
plasma a billion times mutilated. Trampled down.
                            Smashed. Desecrated.
So it is not erosion. Not erosion.
The old woman on the domestic threshold,
bent in two, all in expectation of her son's return from work
                    (he has a job in Grasse,
at Grasset's perfume factory).
                    Smoke dear to one's nostrils,
                    sun-drenched window panes,
                    and you, my dear road—the vehicle
                    for a return home.
                    In lieblicher Bläue
                    die Fenster wie die Thore
                    der Schónheit.... Dichterisch
                    wohnet der Mensch auf dieser

Erdc.... Cold Mother Earth. She waits
for her son's return. Who
waits for me?... No people
except her are in sight.

       —Salut á vous!—she calls loudly
       and confidently. In this excellent
       echo-chamber of the air.

Not erosion. Not hamlets, farms, fire trails, interlacing roads. But—
eczema. But—eczema of the earth, mycosis of the earth. Dec-
             reptitude of the earth. Processes of the earth's
disintegration. Black blight on a stone carcass. The scaling and
                  psoriasis of her scrofulous
child. Also water, even water—certainly—most of all! The digit
on a banknote delights the naive eye. But the
           experienced one sees the water mark: the mark
of eczema, the mark of decrepit nature, alive and not alive.
The old woman in the dark hat
stands on the threshold bent in two
and in a pleasant voice sings:
       And I bore you, son, for eternal dying
       And I raised you, son, for painful rest.
And with her olive stick weaves a concise design in the air.

A stray sheep, staring at me: my worthy sheep, you will rot.
Manure, mycosis, rot, the agony of things living and not living.

V.

"Off with his head."
—The Queen from *Alice in Wonderland*

A pretty innkeeper of La Chèvre d'Or
sits on the porch, her fingers interlaced.
Both of us with a glass of light

wine.

       This trapezoidal
square. And a sycamore
in a casement. A fountain circa 1900,
ascending roads, descending roads

                         crisscrossed.
Along one soldiers descend,
along another soldiers ascend.
60 km., 20 kg. load,
Jean, Pierre, Jacques—and again
Pierre, Jean, Jacques. They march in single-file,
one after another. Where are they being herded?
A rosy inn, yellow tables, sapphire pasture
and blue above our heads. A whiskered old lady
in a gray hat, her head—a toy block set right
on her belly (check to see what Roman artists called this
in the age of decline). She crossed obliquely and vanished.

                               Next a cat, young, fat.
Off with her head—shouts the queen.
The poor soldiers droop under their gear,
wipe off sweat, chance upon the fountain circa 1900,
move out in single file, one of them stumbled,
sighed, farted, fell, his buddies roar,
a bellowing dissonance in a serene concert
of pastoral silence. Off with their heads,
shouts the innkeeper. You are pretty, innkeeper of Cabris,
when you play with your pretty dog Diane,
when you plunge your narrow fingers into her raggy hair,
when you tickle her under her floppy ear,
when your gaze drifts to the pasture
from where dignified, colorful village magi
descended three weeks ago on Epiphany.

                       Now from there a hunter without a leg—
he lost it in the war—a local Don Juan, is coming
for his daily *pastis.* In a smooth Aronde
Mister Fevrard drives up with his Parisian girlfriend.
A setter runs across the square in a chic trot. It scared away

34

a permanent resident, the cat. The owner of the gift shop
returns from her siesta, an ingratiating smile on her flat face.
A stout ninety-year old villager dozes over a liter of red wine.
He breaks wind, the simple soul. Mister Fevrard moves
                                        ten yards farther on.
And all this in the sun, *un après-midi d'hiver.*
38 C. In February, unthinkable
in my country! Where people are born, love, die
in ferocious February. February, wear thick boots
                        and be wary. My country
is a peasant country. In this peasant country
the beautiful innkeeper, a pearl in her ear,
reads Agatha Christie in the doorway. Bored by Diane,
by Agatha, too. In a red Peugeot
a laborer drives up with his heavy-boned family. And again
soldiers pass, one after another, then in pairs,
then in a crowd. How they reek. Of the long road,
and of health. How they will stink
in sickness, in agony. Diane
ran after the last one. Off,
off with his head, shouts the queen Diana Hecate
Luna. In the paled firmament. A shepherd
with his sheep passes by. A cat—a brooding philosopher—
approaches, also the village drunkard, Monsieur Maxime,
a gentle drunkard, kind to people, eager for odd jobs,
slovenly, high-school graduate, in an embroidered skull-cap—
(What fate brought it here from the valleys of Fergana?
where in the whiteness of snows are violet-colored
                                        mountains and the violet
of peaches by the violet of rocks, and the violet tenderly
                        washed in the greens
of a stream, while a rider-philosopher,
a knight in tatters, girt with the scarlet
of Kashmir, passes by in a wild gallop, la ilah ill Allah, passes us
bent down to the dust under dun-colored bags from a
                                labor camp)... And again,
God, those annoying soldiers.

They see the green,
I see snows.
They—in the young sun,
I—in a ferocious winter.
A hunter, a laborer, a bird, a village
orchestra, it returns—
a moustached head, he flails the pavement with a
scissor-kick. Mister Fevrard
gets into the car with his Parisian girlfriend. Off with his head,
shouts the innkeeper.
Whose head? I look around.
Mister Fevrard drove off with his Parisian girlfriend.
Nobody. Alone on the square. With you. Only
with you. Always with you.
Off!—no! No, it happened differently.

VI.

It happened quite differently.
As it does among people. Warmly. Gemütlich. In this way:
Three good buddies, around a samovar with vodka and cucumbers.
Two in suspenders; one in socks, another in slippers,
and the third as if dressed for a ball: a tie, cheap pin-striped
trousers, a frock coat of heavy fabric, lacquered shoes

Let the majordomo rage,
the lackey's looking grim:
we've got you locked up in our cage,
we'll tear you limb from limb
—they sing in chorus, the first even has a quite nice tenor.
They drink, belch, look through
dossier after dossier, piles of dossiers.
"Whore and bandit," scribbles the one in gray socks;

"Off with his head," adds another;
"and brand him a brigand," the one in the tie writes
in a fine hand, like a worthy lawyer.
"A machine of hell?! A masterpiece of Satan?!"—let
the morons unravel it. And we here in a warm stench,
yawning, scratching ourselves, over cucumbers and a samovar—
three buddies. Off— — —
Off!—a voice in the air cries
without lips.—"Whose?"—"A head!"
It is no more. Cut off. Let's go back.
The wind from the sea
gathers us up. And wisps of smoke are fragrant. In the air
pure as a tear. How far one can see! How
tender are the little lights of men,
amen.

                    The green hunter
                    with a vigilant barrel
                    with a dog-mute,
                    at his post.
                    Don't ask him. I've known
                    for a long time.

                         VII.

Satan—and not the Evil one. The Evil one is a devil,
Behemoth, Azazel. No crony to Satan,
not at all, neither kith nor kin.
The other rebelled, yes, but he was rebelling
out of concern for man. Man, it has a proud ring to it,
that's why we rot in this hole, just our tough luck.
As to the devil, he runs errands for God, see
the book of Job, I, 12. From which you should not conclude
God is Evil. On the contrary—Infinitely, Incomprehensibly Good,
which is only a vulgar metaphor of the Incomprehensibly Good, as
it was justly written by Saint Dionysius,

37

the one who had his head cut off.
So don't ask: *unde malum*? Evil is a cognized Good. Perhaps
the reverse. Anyhow, a Good at a lower, so to speak,
stage of *Development*. Why is Satan identified with the devil?—
how should I know? A riddle, at least, at our stage, of
                                        people in the clink. That's
why we are locked up. Our tough luck. Besides, ask
                                Schaff. From the divine
point of view we must be locked up as the spawn of
                                Satan. From the human,
as children of the devil. Confused, as usual, like
                                philosophers. But anyhow—
in the clink.

VIII.

I play la Pétanque. I swear obscenely.
Dominoes with my cronies, backgammon.
I prattle. Grow muddy with drinks. Covered
with sweat, yes, sweat, eczema, mycosis.
My clothes are filthy. No fragrant oils
from Grasse will help; not all the scents of Araby
                                can clean them. Nor
will the breath of my little sister mimosa under the window
undo anything. The sun
looses a parasite in my hair. In its pincers
the tightly caught bone creaks like an old piece of furniture.
It is a high note. It tears heaven apart
from the West to the East. In vain. Nothing
will reach out of there. The Hand is no more. A stone which
does not fall. Hurry up, you gypsy soul. The night
                                is near. Centauresses
defending the Throne, as I wrote at the age of twenty.
                                        Centauresses are no more.
Soon, the screech of an owl. The Hunter is already
at his post,

in a little hat, cockeyed as himself,
with a dog-mute. The urgent sun-fire
calls me from the windows of La Messuguiere tower.
                  Once more turn toward Cabris:
an acropolis in the gold of tiles.
Because the sun bids us farewell in gold
before it departs. Then
in chalky violet
before the night extinguishes it.
Before the night extinguishes us
little fires of human bustle will flare up below.
How good it is to be at home, at last, facing silence.
Purify yourself with censers of sulphur, wool, fire,
fir twigs, in sacral silks
meditate by a candle, with Seneca. *Aetas
serenitatis*; beyond the pass of old age
there is peace. Words, words. Seneca fell from your hand long ago.
You dream, old fogy, you daydream, daydrumdream...

IX.

*"It is the nature of the highest objective
art to be clean. The Muses are maidens."*

—A. Lang, *Homer and Anthropology.*

So beautiful the lungs
are breathless. The hand remembers:
I was a wing.
Blue. The peaks in ruddy
gold. Women of that land —
small olives. On a spacious saucer
wisps of smoke, houses, pastures, roads,
interlacing of roads, o holy diligence
of man. How hot it is! The miracle
of shade returns. A shepherd, sheep, a dog, a ram
all in gilded bells. Olive trees
in twisted benevolence. A cypress—their lone shepherd. A village

39

on a Cabris cliff, protected
by its tiled roofs. And a church, its cypress and shepherd.
Youthful day, youthful times, youthful world.
Birds listen, intently silent. Only a rooster crowing
from below in the hamlet of Spéracèdes. How
hot it is. To die on foreign soil is bitter.
It's sweet to live in France.

X.

For whom is the garden planted?
Who is happy there?
No eyes to be my haven.
How can the heart sustain dying?
Something creeps behind me.
Fear falls away.
What fell in the abyss?
Let the scream resound.
A hand looms above.
A smile hangs suspended.
Don't look at me, my wife.
Son, let go my hand.

XI.

To my wife
on our 35th wedding anniversary.

Enmeshed in the frenzies of praying mantes:
Of Nature's creations, what is more sublime
than a family? Wife, husband, child—
a golden division of the species, the lesser becomes the greater,
and so the tribe renews itself in the festoons of time.

O, mountain stream
Basalt beneath

40

Bedrock of flight
Pendulum-home
Vise of the heart
Lily of the soul
Contralto of quiet
And faithful shroud.
Violet—sorrow,
In winter flakes.
O, you warm earth
Of peaks and valleys!
In sickness and in health
Siamese sister
My Bride.

La Messuguière, January-April, 1962

Translated by Czeslaw Milosz jointly with David Brodsky and Stephen Grad.

DREAMS FROM THE SHORE OF THE MEDITERRANEAN

"Oh, God, I could be bounded in a nutshell
And count myself a king of infinite
Space, were it not that I have bad dreams."
                —Hamlet

"The Lord constantly punished us and constantly terrified us
With fires, the black death, the witch of hunger,
With eyes of unknown stars, horrible dreams
And princes mad at our freedom."
            —Slowacki. *Prince Michael of Tver.*

1.

Using both hands, my senses in rapt attention, gently,
                     you see, doctor,
I always carried before me, like a lantern, a cage
                         made of young reeds
and a butterfly circled in it, whose name I don't know.
Not so much white as woven of light, only the ribbing
was thick, not transparent. I say "lantern" for indeed it illuminated
the road before me. Yes, that was night, but made radiant dawn
by the butterfly. And the road led through oily tidelands, true,
                  shallow, but there your leg bogs and sloshes.
Their colors brought to mind pigeons' throats when
                      after my nightly rounds
of the city, I returned to my warm home at daybreak,
                 a sturdy Ahasver
chased by a judgment never proclaimed but almost always
                    an inkling. And you know,
I was so deep in thought, so bewildered by the
                  excess of forebodings,
that my butterfly broke away from me. With the
                 strength of an eagle.
Speeding at first like a stone, not down—up. Then moving
                 to the West. But since I
pursued my opposing way, it suddenly turned and
                again started to circle

near me, rotating faster, much more angrily,
oh, it even crowed once or twice, though till now had
                              been mortally silent.
This, doctor, was repeated exactly three times. In vain, at home
my mother waited for me, under her starched sheet; I had to fulfill
the ancient duty of a son. So my butterfly, no more butterfly,
—now a bird, gave up on me with a wave of its broad wing
and seemed to be not angry, not at all, just in despair. About me.
And flew off, for ever. So now, doctor,
must I for ever do without the lantern? And what does
                              that dream mean, doctor?
But please, this time, no sex. That's not what I need:
                              what I need is breath
nourishing, for my lungs, a light for my heart,
                              earthly food for my eyes.
For it's dark, the road leads through suffocating marshes,
                    and I am left without lantern, without wings,
without the cage, and I really don't know what to
                              do with my freedom
when I no longer have my butterfly?

                    2.

I spent the early years of my youth
in the belly of a fish. From the old species
Balistes Capricus. I was not quite
thirteen, when it spat me out. Indeed, in a fine parabola.
What a trip!
                    I still haven't come to my senses
after the shock of birth. It seemed the trajectory
would never reach its goal!
I scared gulls, oh, not those sweet ones, forever sweet to us
our native swallows. My left leg caught on a chimney
tall and leaning unnaturally—ship after ship,
battleships, schooners. From dazzling upper decks
I was oberved through binoculars. Radiantly naked

ladies in maritime hairdoes, laden with jewels,
induced in me a state of shame. After all the more so since I myself
was naked. *Passons*. So, it's a seaport. Tyre? Sidon? Perhaps
Syracuse? Yet, uncertain, I ask
its name. How they started shouting! Waving their arms!
Undoing spells! (in contortions and secretly, I know this,
I practised it myself). How they were scat-ter-ing! So where am I,
for Heaven's sake? those heavy tits, those
puppet faces, those colored wigs exposed behind windowpanes
to the glare? Not one of them winks, though their eyes incessantly
turn. Pretty, those eyes, one green, the other hazel. And
before her, and her, and her
a stein. Or else *un bock*. Like on rue Blondel, for two francs.
Arrogant Bruno caught a glass through the windowpane,
leans his horselike head, sips, puts it aside,
"good beah," smacks his lips, falls, he will die in labor-camp
agony, in the distant, oh, how distant North. Poor
woodcutter. Let's recite
a quick prayer for him. A gang of woodcutters returns
from work. "A bell rings for prayers...",
they sing. I am tired of all this. Where is my fish?
Back there, right now!
I inquire. All of you are deaf and dumb in this city.
In the damned city. In this city
you are damned. In a sentenced city. For ever. "Order a
procession," I say imperiously
to the mayor. "Let them solemnly circle the walls,
purify with incense
the unclean gates, as it is Februarius, the month of expiation."
Deaf as a post, he stands, breast to pointed breasts, with his naked,
jewel-laden wench. Everybody here with his naked wench.
Only I'm alone. Alone
I loiter in these tortuous, damned little streets.
And everything began
so promisingly: Swallows in flight, *Kinder an
Reinheit*! So I sit down,
spent, in a gutter. This is Sidon. *Vicolo d'Amor*

Perfetto. Luminous,
white skeletons of ships, of sailboats, all the purchasable colors
from postcards. Of a Sentenced city.
     So I squat under the bougainvillea, the
                  one from the quarries
where naked Artemises in maritime hairdoes, laden with jewels,
shot at us with golden bows, looking at our agony
                  from above. At agony—
always from above. When not seen from above, what is agony?
                  One cloud curiously white
floats away.

3.

Tue-les, howls the mob. *Ausrotten,*
screeches a parrot in a white jabot;
an English tailored suit; grayish
bangs; she is slender, bony and chic;
her eye—a flaring sapphire against gray flannel.
Tue-les—howls the mob. How hard it is
to move my legs. Though conversations of one's
                  countrymen are sweet,
let us look up their sleeves. *Ausrotten,* screeches
a lady with a parrot's head, she slipped into
the crowd undulating on the sidewalks, but in the empty
middle of the roadway—it's me, only me, a little
Jew a poor Algerian—me again, me,
until it's hard to bear. She: *ausrotten.* The others
                  are already hoarse.
A warm hand on my forehead: "Wake up." Nothing equals
a loving hand on your forehead. But still so much road
before me. Now a flower with the face of a bestial child.
Ausrotten! And birds are silent. And the Hunter
listens with a steel gun barrel—a phallic symbol? By the way,
it it possible to make one's own psychoanalysis while sleeping?
Once I succeeded.... In the "Siberia" of the Warsaw neurology

clinic, where the epileptic Y*** kept jumping up
and throwing his arm wildly. *Tue-les*, they howled then
outside the window. Old M***'s death rattle came from above his
hanging jaw, a withered Ramses, he will die in the morning
under the loudspeaker which will splutter sweet

                                     cream of wheat for the hog
and a plump wench will scratch her unsleepy behind

                        bandaging with her other hand that unruly
jaw. But you were near by! Kill, kill, rattled

                           the mob outside the window.

               And birds are silent. And in the mounains
the Hunter. But you are with me, now nothing can

                    happen to us. Let's go.
How difficult it is to lift my leg. *Ausrotten*, screeches

                    the parrot in the jabot.

Let's go on. How easy it is
to descend uphill.

                         4.

              To my sisters, Seda and Cesia

At the Greek's behind the shop window, the sea—sponges, lobsters—
the top sky high. On display cakes
with pointed bellies, tawny, olive, coral-red.
Behind the shop window my three sisters walk, one after the other.
How far will they get?—I fall into meditation. Thus, behind

                    the shop window, the sea.
We dropped in at The Greek's for a moment. But

                the sea, obnoxious sea, the top sky high,
its layers innumerable. And they are so
wavy. Cakes, yes: $1, \sqrt{-7}, \text{alef}^0, : 0$.
I am cheating, I know. Whereas the Greek makes

                      change honestly: three kopeks—
coppers, I feel their taste in my fingertips—only this was missing
to get shoved by the scruff to my childhood's first dreams!
So I dream. I dream *ergo* I sleep. All the better.

I dream in Eastman—
color. What did Askanas call this? The second system—but of
what? I don't remember.
I prattle and my three sisters don't stop hurting their
feet. The fourth one,
an adolescent mimosa, waits downstairs, by
the door. Let Ola lead me
out of the sea. Let us sail away. On little sleighs.
In the park, of Ujazdów,
I will look at the swans, sob. My hair flying
from my skull—where I have as a permanent resident
a centenarian lobster,
my little contemporary, striped with sapphire and minium—
will surface, a silver medusa, alone and without me.

5.

To Prof. dr. Zdislaw Askanas

The snow on my eyes has melted, bony fingers on my neck
have turned into a necklace. Then You, dear, came running
drawn by a passerby's shout beyond the window. What can he know,
a passerby on this earth of the settled? I remember,
a braggart stag, proud of his necklace,
a changing rainbow in sunny dew,
walked through Waliców, and in a window open to Summer
fragrance, to an array of lilacs and of chestnut trees in bloom
a boy was sitting. He wore a skullcap,
his black eyes stared nowhere. I remember,
the stag mocked, he said something so jeeringly
that the child withdrew into the room,
insulted.
Inside there was a bed, on it a form
absolutely horizontal (as somewhere in Rembrandt).
That stag, what did he know? He was a passerby on this earth
of the settled. Oh, he knew enough, when he was slowly walking
home. What could be done? He wept. The necklace

47

chokes my throat. Break it, let the bone beads
scatter. Years, places, dark
attachments, they also scatter.
Then the Hunter arrives, drawn by a shout,
and wighs on his hand all your poor treasures,
as if he wanted to return them to you. But he only looks
and weighs, one after the other, and drops one
                    after the other in the dust of the street.
The snow on your eyes already melted, you may wake up.

6.

When I meet an elephant, I shall ask him for his doctor's address.
I could also ask my neighbor, a palm tree, it's
                              thick-skinned enough,
but I know: it won't even mutter back, it slights me.
This makes me so uneasy! Thin-skinned, I haven't
                              gone out of the house
for ages, though—ah! I am lured
by les Grands Boulevards. Most of all on Sunday,
in the late afternoon, in the heat of Summer,
                              when even the tourists
have taken shelter in their nests by the sea. I simply love the mobs
swarming out of their tenements. Young mothers with
                              sleepy kids, chic salesmen,
stately married couples and ethereal girls from brainless
streets, colorful dayflies. Neon lights from movie-houses
caress them all with the luster of brief happiness.
Which is refused to me. I've locked myself in a narrow
cage at my hotel and so days and years pass me by.
                              No, a hundred times no,
I don't want them looking through my skin at my shame:
those tangles, veinings, those coils, nervures, those textures—
a non-figurative painting in which every gaper
will see what suits him: one—flotillas dragging nets, another—
nightmares with snouts telescoped into dogs', frogs' paws.

48

                              Somebody else—
a dump where a scavenger, once the pearl of bordelloes,
rakes out with a stick her poor treasures. Or, for a change—
streams, Euphratean tributaries, five-branched rivers
                              veining black earth, Or—
a lode of gneiss, marbled with lime, yellow clay, carnelian.
And, somebody very cruel—a work of a mad
                              craftsman, a mute organ
which no one has ever played and on which nothing
                              will ever be played.

                              7.

                    To André and Françoise

              "*L'immense baleine se nourrit de minuscules
              Copepodes et Schizopodes.*"
                    —H. Decugis. *Le Vieillissement du Monde Vivant*

The night watchman walked into the well-heated house, ringing
his keys and sat down on the King's bed. They play cards.
Early morning. Before the window a red vine streams down
curtain-like, incessantly, and fences us from
savage passersby in skins: they are Mongols, they shoot
their matchlock muskets at little birds which this night inhabited
the King's dreams. The most wicked of the King's daughters,
now an Amazon, gambols under the surface of ponds and her two
greyhounds chase a carp. In its old eyes,
thanks to a foolish arrangement of Nature, is reflected
the eidolon of the King, when he plays cards with the watchman,
his most faithful chamberlain. With him every night,
after he wakes up, before he falls asleep again, the King strolls
back and forth, back and forth, in front of his palace
which trembles like jelly, though the structure
is substantial. What do they talk about? What do they gamble for?
Me, no doubt. Perhaps. Though after all I am

                              49

less than a snail and a tenant of His Majesty's grass
only by His favor. Sometimes they invite me in
for a meal i.e. a feast. One crunches nice geese in a sauce
of sour beets, stuffed with snails from the same royal garden.
Savage passersby shoot muskets, blow twisted horns,
which does not disturb at all the festive eclogues at our table.
Beyond a wine-colored curtain the light of a tallow candle,
the only one here: thrifty housekeeping and
                                        family warmth is provided,
o yes. Right now passersby, a band, girls from Les Halles
will enter. I will slip down along the drooping tablecloth
under the table where cards are scattered. There I shall wait out
December, drunkards' hiccups, a flight, with a tremolo of fifes,
to the moon, lack of dough, manifestations of the people
and the mistral which constantly drones in this region.
In my region, not at all. And the trees are different, more sturdy,
in other words: more humane. And they cast a denser shade,
allowing the moss to spread softly under noiseless steps
of the Hunter. While in their crowns one can hide
and be secure. Though to be sure, here under the table
the dogs will do me no harm either. They yawn.
That's fine.

8.

For Czeslaw Milosz

They who support my arm, will they be stopped by the aroma
of vineyards? A huge bell of air—will they hear in their lungs
its silver sound? Now only my lungs feel the spring youthfully,
they alone sate themselves with the young rustling of the
                                        day over the stream
of herbs and seas. But they, their grasp never
                                slackens and their gaze
is stony. An imaginable deer darts before us, hides in a thicket,
spots flash by in the grass, now stands in sunlight
                                        by a waterhole

50

and looks at the bony shells of its horns bathed
In the golden flecks of the stream. But you must move on.
                              Forward or backward—I don't know.
They who guide by the arm and have a stony gaze.
                              Yet they too should see
these stones all around! Should slacken their grip, should be swayed
by the rocks' expression: of surprise? adoration? menace?
These gestures of sacrificers, of the sacrificed, of
                              orantes! Here a knight,
weary unto death, who returned from a long war, rested his head
against the peak of his house long since turned to stone, where dwell
moss and desolation, a flighty lizard, where the locust, slim dancer,
has sped to the hunt from a heavy cocoon, having
                              stuck it with saliva
onto calcite, ages would pass and not unglue it, a sturdy buck
would gobble the young and the gnawed nest
                              endures. Like the ruins
of a City. They who lead by the arm are angels.
                              Surely angels. Oh, not the kind
That dive from above. Neither the breath, so pure,
                              of those from above
nor the silver tone of their trumpets will trouble them who guide me.
They are messengers, only messengers, nothing more, their route
traced from the beginning of time. Let's go on. Let's trample
moss, lizards, let's blister our feet on the pumice of the road
through the petrified sands of deserts, let's mark
                              with a bloody zigzag
a trail for others. Let him who wants to,
flap his wing, it's powerless, but this gives the soul élan.
Let's pass Artemises by the stream, laundresses,
                              maybe Greek, or Jewish.
The clatter of paddles animates Nature. It lauds
                              her, daughter of Dione.
Here everything lauds the daughter of Dione. Let
                              me come near the well,
let me look into the eyes of Rachel. But they who guide me
will not swerve from the road. And I, too, keep in mind

51

the adventure of a man who preceded me. He did
                        not turn into salt but—
oh, the heart's eternal sorrow!
                        Owls' eyes in the alders which
                        we pass. And the eyes
of a peacock's tail. Peacocks ceased screeching
                        their strangled complaint.
For everything fell silent at once out of pity:
                        looking on your *disgrace*.
Yes, since you are dragged, towed, by your hair, your legs.
The eyes, all the eyes are averted and now only silence
lauds the daughter of Dione. Who eternally rises from the seas,
radiant. High is such praise. But you do not hear
that graceful silence. To the brim of memory
                        you are full of voices.
Voices from the house, voices from the garden, voices
                        from the forest, voices
from above you—they are gone and yet remain
                        and will not go away
even when the abortive human species disappears;
                        they will enter into
swallows, mosses, insects, stones, nothingness
                        if necessary. Into silence
which is the voice of the voice primeval.
                        They, angels, who drag you, stone
is not in their eyes, their eyes in truth are tender and human,
but their eyes see only stone.
                        Their blood does not trace their route
and their eyes are not stone, not at all, they are unfathomable,
the same and changing, tender human eyes. But they
                        see only one thing: the stone of your heart.
Besides, everything lauds the daughter of Dione who eternally
emerges from the seas, radiant, her hair luxuriously curled.
But your ears are tightly sealed with beeswax.
                        Sealed against silence.
Yet something penetrates them: the distant creaking
                        of a peasant cart.

And peasant chatter echoing from the forest,
those voices untaught, not taught by Nature—
as even minerals, even a mole, even blades of grass are—
but not our churlish, dear tender peasant
voices:
        That's my gravediggers singing.

La Messuguière, Cabris, February-March, 1962
Translated by Czeslaw Milosz and Richard Lourie

A FEW AUTHOR'S NOTES TO "SONGS OF A WANDERER"

Second Song

. . . *into the stone world:* Préalpes de Grasse. Hard limestone from the early Jurassic age; later stratifications of chalk, gypsum, sand; marine deposits from the Pliocene age. Here and there the wavy profile of many formations is exposed. Landslides of flint, porous blocks of volcanic lava, metamorphic rocks, gneiss veined with black mica; below, nummolite stratifications, soft sandstone. The bas-relief of the terrain is boldly variegated in a state of *becoming,* of incompleteness visible to the naked eye. The folds of the mountains, overlapping, eroded by labyrinthine ravines and gorges of the streams Siagne and Loup encircle large plateaus and plains with their rings open to the sea. Covered by a mass of luxuriant greenery right up to the tall summits of the cliffs; of trees, the olive, and low evergreen cork oaks and many varieties of acacias predominate; here and there, clumps of stone pine, no lack of poplars, alders, figs and cypress trees; myrtles, hard, steel-green agaves; a countless abundance of shrubs and herbs—everything on that ungrateful soil, subject to chemical and physical erosion, fertilized by the toil of so many generations. The eagles' nests of old villages—small fortified towns. The air so clear that on calm mornings the shores of Corsica, about 200 kilometers away, become visible and the scale of light values surpasses every painter's palette.

On the other hand, beyond the nearest pass is another world: the cupola-like profile of the Trias, bare mountains with snow on the ridges of their peaks, here and there the olive-drab smudges of lichens and dwarf mountain pine, the barren Provence. Amphitheaters of volcanic rock, also perhaps of Achean megaliths—with forms so chimerical they could serve as the scenery for a *Walpurgisnacht.* There—the turbullent, multiform bulk of the becoming world, here—the monotonous agony of space.

Fourth Song

. . . by the Vengeful Hand (Jehovah's): a not sufficiently exact translation of "Beyod hazoko", containing the idea of might and violence, but certainly of vengeance as well.

. . . Grasse: an old, picturesque town 18 kilometers from the sea. At present its chief industry is perfumes.

. . . *In lieblicher Bläue*: a poem by Friedrich Hölderlin from his late period (vol. VI, Propyläen-Verlag) beginning with these words.

. . . in a dark hat: very old women sometimes seem the sole inhabitants of Cabris (those younger and the men work in Grasse): they never show themselves outside the house except when wearing a hat; straw, flat, with a wide brim, dark gray or gray-brown patined by rain and time—to a stranger it makes an impression like a uniform for those preparing for death.

Fifth Song

A small scene from life, pedantically realistic with the interpolation of an inner monologue by the author. Only the names have been changed.

. . . magi descended: in the last few years the ancient procession of the Three

Kings in medieval Provençal costumes has been resumed here.

. . . Diana Hecate Luna: the triple incarnation of Artemis. NB the reminiscence from *Delie* (XIII: "Like Hecate you make me err") by Maurice Scève, a great poet of the XVI century. To distinguish her (or not) from the three-headed Hecate-Persephone of Hades.

. . . from the valleys of Fergana: Molotovobad, in Uzbekistan, where the author found himself in the spring of 1942. The configuration of mountainous terrain, the physiognomy of the flora (in the sense used by W. von Humboldt, *Ansichten der Natur*) its general synoptic looks, trees in pathetic gesticulations, the dramatic "happenings" of the landscape, the clarity of the air, the multigrade intensity of the light —all that, strange thing, brings to mind the place in Provence in which the present verses were written.

Sixth Song

cf. the speech of A. Shelepin, the chief of the Security Police of the USSR, at the XXII Congress. Cit. "Cahiers du Communisme," No. 12, 1961, p. 291: "Staline écrivit sur cette lettre (of the imprisoned general Jakir): 'scélérat et prostitue,' Voroshilov ajouta: 'définition parfaîtement exacte' . . . Kaganovitsch 'ecrivit encore: 'Au traître, à la crapule et (suit un mot obscène) un seul chatîment: la mort.' "

Seventh Song

. . . St. Dionysius: the pseudo-Areopagite, identified by church tradition with the martyr and first bishop of Paris (Lutetia), who is depicted with his own cut-off head in his hand. According to his theological treatise *De divinis nominibus* evil is only the tendency of finite things to non-being; speaking metaphorically: "a zero, itself not existing, as a multiplier of any being gives zero." Since Being is indestructible, even the devil therefore cannot be immanently evil, for he would cease to be. In a word, evil is non-being (non-ens), but the temporal evil which we endure: our own sufferings, those inflicted by others, illnesses—exists in our finite would exclusively in so far as it is good.

Eighth Song

. . . I swear obscenely, play backgammon: cf. Machiavelli's letter of Francesco Vettori: "... Twilight falls, I return home from the tavern, I throw off my filthy rags, dress myself in regally sacral silks, to hold intercourse with the ancients in the still of the library..."

. . . Centauresses defending the Throne: cf. my book, *I From One Side and I From the Other Side of My Pug-Iron Stove,* Warsaw, 1920.

. . . La Messuguière: estate near Cabris, a foundation for French intellectuals established by Andrée Vienot, where these verses were written.

. . . of sulphur, wool: a Roman ritual of purification and expiation *(februatio).*

Eleventh Song

. . . the golden division: the whole is to the greater part as it is to the smaller:

$$\frac{a + b}{a} = \frac{a}{b}$$

From antiquity it ranks as the most harmonious arrangement, used with plea-
sure in architecture, in art and also in crystals, in the morphology of plants and even
of numerous sea-creatures, and in the form of the human body. (Luca Pacioli, in the
treatise *De divina Proportione,* 1509, calls it devine. Hambridge in *Dynamic Sym-
metry* demonstrates that it makes possible the creation of further divisions with the
preservation   of an identical morphological theme. NB: this information is taken
from the work of M. C. Ghyka, *La Proportion dans les arts plastiques,* in L'Encyclo-
pédie Française, Vol. XVI.)

A FEW NOTES TO "THE DREAMS"

Second Dream

. . . *Balistes Capricus:* a fish from the family *Balistides.* I repeat in a free para-
phrase what de Lacépède has written about it (*Histoire Naturelle,* vol. II, Paris,
1836): In the cruel world of fish and sea monsters, the balistides are distinguished by
a philosophic gentleness. They are armoured, indeed they know how to defend themselves, but they themselves do not attack, their food is not other fish: they do not
sow terror, nor are they subject to it. Nature has granted them a rare charm, the gift
of the light and the warmth of hot seas, colors pleasing to the eye and properly con-
trasted. The Mediterranean variety of *Balistes Capricus* is light violet, has the reflexes
of a pigeon's throat, incrustations of azure and aquamarine, vermillion fins; its large
eyes encircled in bright yellow are "like sapphires in a golden setting." The English
calls their less conspicuous variety old wife. Their bellies are particularly extendable
which makes it easy for them to fill with air, and consequently gives them mobility
and manoeuvrability in diving. Their flesh is poisonous.
. . . Bruno: Bruno Jasienski in Paris in 1926.
. . . the bell rings for prayers, mother calls for supper, time to go home now,
they're calling us home now": from the song "Though the Storm Roars Around Us,"
sung by Poles in prisons and in remote Soviet labor camps.
. . . "Kinder an Reinheit": from Holderin's poem *In lieblicher Bläue...*
. . . "Vicolo d'Amor Perfetto": a filthy alley in Genoa with old, gray-haired
prostitutes.
. . . the bougenvillea, the one from the quarries: a real one, beautifully devel-
oped, at the exit of the deep quarries (Latomia del Paradiso) in Syracuse. In the 5th
century B.C., the Athenian youth taken into slavery perished there beneath a scorch-
ing sun (cf. Thucydides, *The Peloponesian War*). This was certainly the first extermination camp in history. Now—it is a paradise of birds and vegetation.

Third Dream

. . . "In Siberia": thus the patients reviled the neurology ward at the Infant Je-
sus Hospital in Warsaw where the author was a patient in the beginning of 1953.
. . . under the loudspeaker: at that time, in hospital wards loudspeakers were
obligatory from morning until 10:00 in the evening.

Fourth Dream

. . . at the Greek's: before 1914, a bakery popular in Warsaw, owned by

57

Greeks who also engaged in peddling sponges.

Fifth Dream

. . . somewhere in Rembrandt: in the National Museum in Brussels a painting by Rembrandt depicting a dead woman.

Eighth Dream

. . . the rocks' expression: a stone amphitheater with fantastic shapes on the road to St. Vallier, possibly megaliths of very ancient ritual site.
. . . the daughter of Dione: Aphrodite.
. . . Everything lauds: from the Orphic hymns.
. . . the adventure of a man: Orpheus, who could accompany Eurydice from Hades on the condition—which wasn't fulfilled—that he did not look her in the eye.